STO ✓

JUL 2 8 1989
4/92-3

FRIENDS
OF ACPL

J362.8
BERRY
ALERTING KIDS TO THE DANGER
OF KIDNAPPING

ALERTING KIDS TO THE DANGER OF KIDNAPPING

WRITTEN BY JOY BERRY
Pictures by Bartholomew

WORD

Educational Products Division
Waco, Texas 76796

Allen County Public Library
Ft. Wayne, Indiana

Executive Producer: Ron Berry
Producer: Marilyn Berry
Designer: Abigail Johnston
Contributing Editors: Nancy Cochran, Susan Motycka
Editor: Kate Dickey
Consultants: Ellen Klarberg, Kathleen McBride

Copyright ©1984 by Joy Berry. All rights reserved.
Published by arrangement with Living Skills Press by the
Educational Products Division of Word, Incorporated,
4800 W. Waco Drive, Waco, Texas 76796.

Printed in the United States of America

ISBN: 0-8499-8223-5

4567898 KP 987654321

Attention Parents and Teachers

What you don't know CAN hurt you!

People used to believe that children should be kept ignorant for their own sake. In our rapidly changing world, this simply isn't realistic any more. Your children need to know as much as they can about life and its **danger zones.** Since their imaginations can create fantasies worse than any actual situation, they need correct and comprehensible information. The more children know, the better they will be able to protect themselves should they encounter a dangerous situation.

All responsible, caring adults want children to be safe. Unfortunately, our society is becoming increasingly unsafe for children. Young people are being kidnapped at a frightening rate. The most recent statistics estimate that

- 1.8 million children are reported missing each year.
- 20,000 to 50,000 of the missing children are the victims of foul play, such as kidnapping by strangers.
- 8,000 of these children are never found.

Statistics also show that kidnapping is not just a concern of wealthy families whose children are seized and held for large ransoms. Children from families of every income level are kidnapped. The problem affects all parents, guardians, teachers, and other adults who are responsible for the care of children.

What can you do to help prevent these senseless and abhorrent incidents? Give your children the information they need to avoid being kidnapped. This book provides simple explanations that children can understand. It lists preventive measures along with practical steps to take in a dangerous situation.

Read this book with your children and make sure they understand it. Ask them if they have any questions. Then answer their questions openly and honestly. By doing these things, you are taking an essential step toward ensuring your children's safety. Their awareness of the problem and their knowledge of precautionary techniques can be their best protection.

The back of this book contains important information for parents and teachers. This section includes safety guidelines that you can follow to help protect your children.

This material is not intended to frighten you or your children. The point of this book is to turn fear into healthy caution and to empower young people to remain safe, happy, and free.

Most of the people in the world are good people.
They are kind and helpful.
This is why you are safe <u>most</u> of the time.

However, there are a few people who have serious problems.
These people can be harmful.
This is why you are not safe <u>all</u> of the time.

You need to protect yourself against
the few harmful people in the world.
Kidnapping is one of the harmful experiences
you need to avoid.

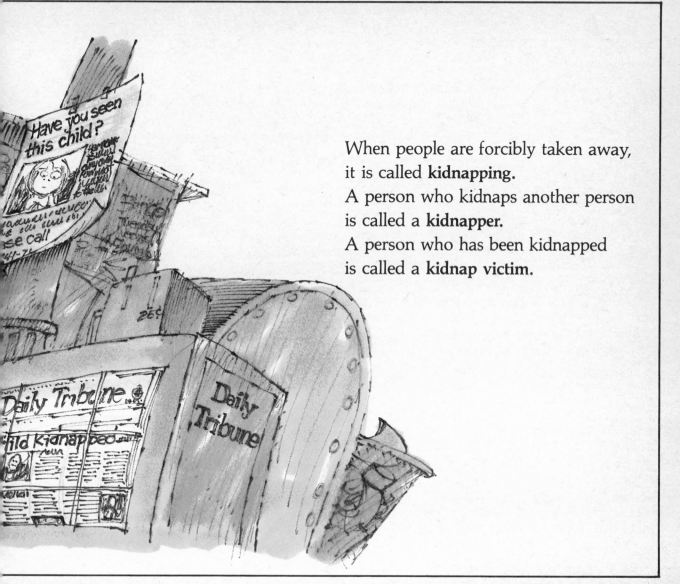

When people are forcibly taken away,
it is called **kidnapping**.
A person who kidnaps another person
is called a **kidnapper**.
A person who has been kidnapped
is called a **kidnap victim**.

There are several reasons why
a few troubled people kidnap others.

Some people **want children** and do not have a way of getting them.
Some of these people may kidnap another person's child
and pretend that the child is their own.

Some people **are lonely.**
Some of these people may kidnap a person
so that they can have a companion.

I'm so
LONELY!

Some people **need a worker.**
These people may kidnap someone
and force the person
to do work for them.

I need someone to do this work.

Some people **want money.**
These people may kidnap
someone and then say that
they will not return the
person unless they are given
some money. The money
that a kidnapper demands is
called a **ransom.**

Some people **are angry**
and want to get back at someone for
whatever has upset them. They express their
anger by kidnapping a person.

Some people are **sexual abusers.**
These people kidnap someone so that they
can have sexual contact with the person.

There are many things kidnappers do to get
children to go with them.

1. BRIBES
Some kidnappers bribe children.
They give children gifts or
make promises to do favors
so the children will go away with them.

Candy, money, and surprises are common bribes.
Another common bribe is
the promise to take children
to a very special place
where the children will have a lot of fun.

13

I'm going the same way you are. How about letting me give you a ride?

2. TRICKS
Some kidnappers trick children. They tell children convincing lies. The lies make the children believe that it is OK to go away with the kidnapper. Here are some common lies kidnappers tell children to trick them.

I'll walk.

15

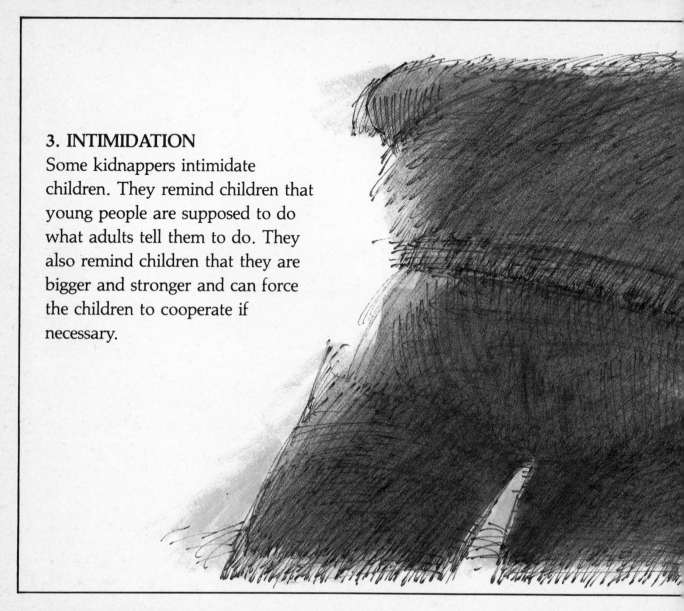

3. INTIMIDATION

Some kidnappers intimidate children. They remind children that young people are supposed to do what adults tell them to do. They also remind children that they are bigger and stronger and can force the children to cooperate if necessary.

4. FORCE

Some kidnappers use their strength to overpower children. They restrain children to make the children go away with them.

There are six things that make it easy for kidnappers to kidnap someone.

1. Kidnapping is easier when **children are not supervised by adults.**
This is because adults are not available
to protect the children and
keep them from going away with kidnappers.

2. Kidnapping is easier when **no one knows where the children are.**
This is because families and friends might assume that everything is OK
when they do not hear from the children.
By the time they begin to wonder and worry,
it is often too late to find the kidnappers or the children.

3. Kidnapping is easier when **children are alone.**
This is because there is no one to help the
children get away from the kidnappers.
There is no one to report the
kidnapping and get help for the children.

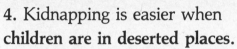

4. Kidnapping is easier when
children are in deserted places.
This is because there is no one around to stop
the kidnappers from taking the children.
There is no one to report the incident
and get help.

It sure is
quiet around
here.

5. Kidnapping is easier when
children are in public places after dark.
This is because the kidnappers can
sneak up and overpower the children.
It is difficult for other people
to see and report what has happened.

Want a ride home?

6. Kidnapping is easier when **children are not cautious.** This is because the children may be cooperative instead of resistant. The children may go willingly or allow the kidnappers to do whatever they want to do.

You can avoid being kidnapped by doing these six things.

1. Wherever you are, **make sure there is an adult close by** who can reach you and help you immediately.
If you are ever left at home alone,
make sure you know
what adult you are to contact
in case of an emergency.

I'll be gone for only one hour. If you need help, call Ms. Parker next door.

Bye!

If you are ever lost, find a trustworthy adult,
such as a police officer, security officer, or sales clerk,
and ask that adult to help you.

You should be able to give this information
to anyone who is helping you when you are
separated from your parents or guardians:
- your full name
- your address
- your telephone number, including your area code
- your parents' or guardians' full names
- the names and addresses of the places
  where your parents or guardians work
- their telephone numbers

You may not be able to find someone to help you.
In this case, you will need to know
how to make a collect call from a pay telephone.
This is so you can call your parents or
guardians at home or at work.

Operator, I'd like to make a collect call.

Don't forget to get your coins back.

2. Make sure your parents or guardians know exactly where you are and what you will be doing at all times. Before you leave home, answer these questions:

- Where will you be? What is the name, address, and telephone number of the place?
- What will you be doing?
- How will you get there? Who will take you? Will you be walking or riding your bike?
- When do you plan to return? Who will bring you home?

<u>When you leave home,</u> go directly to the place where you said you would be going, and stay there.

- If you decide to go somewhere else on the way, call your parents or guardians and tell them where you are.
- If you decide to go to another place after you have reached your destination, call your parents or guardians and tell them where you will be.

Dad, Susan and I are going over to Mary's house.

Drat. I like Susan's house. She's got cats.

- If it is necessary for you
  to change your route in any way,
  let your parents or guardians know.
- Be home when you say you will be home.
- If you are going to be late,
  call and let your parents or guardians
  know why you will be late and
  when you will be home.

I've got to leave.
I said I'd be home
at 4:30.

Good-bye!

3. Avoid going places alone.
Make sure there is at least one other person
with you wherever you go.

4. Avoid being in deserted places.
If you must pass through a deserted area,
make sure an adult or another person is with you.
Then proceed cautiously and quickly.

5. Avoid being in dark places,
such as tunnels, alleys, and covered walkways.

Avoid being outside after dark.

We'd better hurry if we're going to make it home before dark.

6. Be extremely careful around strangers
(people you do not know).
If you are not with an adult,
  • do not talk to strangers,
  • do not take **anything** from strangers, and
  • do not let strangers touch you.

If you are home alone,
- do not open the door for a stranger,
- do not allow a stranger in your house, and
- do not tell anyone who calls on the telephone that you are home alone.

My mother can't come to the phone right now. Can I take a message?

Do they want to talk to me?

There are several things you can do
if a stranger approaches you.

1. Say "No!" to anything a stranger asks you to do.

2. Run away if the stranger tries to touch you.

3. Scream for help if a stranger tries to grab you.
Say, "Help me, I am being kidnapped!"
Say this so that people will not think
you are just throwing a tantrum.

4. Tell your parents or guardians about <u>any</u> stranger who approaches you.
If necessary, your parents or guardians will report the incident to the police. They may ask you to describe the person who approached you. You may need to tell them
   - what the person looked like,
   - what the person was wearing, and
   - what kind of vehicle the person was driving.

Remember, it's always a good idea to talk to your parents or guardians if you have any questions about how to keep yourself safe from kidnapping.

If you are ever kidnapped, try to find a trustworthy adult. Ask the adult to help you get to the nearest police station.

If you cannot get to the police station, try to get to a telephone. Dial "O" for the operator. Ask the operator to connect you with the police department. You will need to tell the police your name and where you are. If you do not know where you are, tell the police the number of the telephone you are using. If you do not know the number, stay on the telephone long enough for the police to locate you.

Try to stay where you are until the police come and get you to take you home.

Out of the millions of young people in the world only some are kidnapped.

BE CAREFUL AND STAY SAFE!

48

Important Information for Parents and Teachers

To Fight or Not to Fight

A decision all parents must make is whether to teach their children to aggressively defend themselves against attackers. There are two schools of thought on this.

1. By kicking, hitting, and biting, kids can startle their attacker and get away.
2. Such actions only anger the attacker and could cause children to be hurt.

This book does not advocate aggressive self-defense for the following reasons:

- Keeping the assault as nonviolent as possible reduces the chance of the child getting hurt or even killed.
- Since the majority of assaults on children are nonviolent, assertive behavior such as saying "no" and running away is more appropriate than fighting.
- There is no way of knowing whether or not an attacker has a weapon. Fighting back could cause the attacker to react by using a weapon that is concealed.
- Self-defense training can give children a false sense of security. Instead of being cautious, they might think they can get out of any dangerous situation by fighting.

Safety Measures

Here are some things you can do **with your children** to protect them from being kidnapped.

- Make a supply of homemade "location reports" using the questions on page 30. Have your children fill out a report before they leave the house.
- Urge your children to call you when they reach their destination. Make sure they have change with them for using a pay phone.

- Set up a secret code word known only by you, your children, and the person who is authorized by you to transport your children. The code word can assure your children that the person who approaches them has been given permission to transport them.
- Have your children practice calling the operator and police for assistance.
- Teach your children how to describe people by comparison. For example, is a person taller than Daddy? Is a person's hair darker or lighter than Mommy's? Accurate descriptions are important when reporting an incident.
- Make a game out of reading and remembering license plates when traveling. Be sure to have your children take note of states as well as numbers. This will help your children remember a license plate if they need to report one.
- Prepare your children by role playing various "kidnapping scenes" with them. This will teach them to respond to dangerous situations appropriately.
- Encourage your children to trust their intuition and react assertively when a situation does not "feel right" to them. Even if your children overreact, it's better to be safe than sorry.

Here are some things that **you** can do to protect your children from being kidnapped.

- Do not put your children's names on the outside of their clothing or possessions. Kidnappers can easily disarm children by calling them by name.
- Make a mental note of what your children are wearing when they leave the house. A description of their clothing can help in their identification and rescue.
- Make arrangements with your children's school to call you if your children are absent.